Surviving the Censor

The Unspoken Words of Osip Mandelstam

Surviving the Censor

The Unspoken Words of Osip Mandelstam

Rafi Aaron

Seraphim Editions

The poem "Voronezh" was selected by Tim Lilburn as a winning entry in *Grain* magazine's prose poetry competition in 2003; "Mandelstam—A Biography," "The Years of Silence," "Living My Death," and the "The Last Poem" were shortlisted for the 2003 National Magazine Awards and were first published in *ARC*, as was "Natasha Shtempel and the Evacuation of Voronezh," which was a finalist and editor's choice in the 2003 Poem of the Year Competition; other poems in this book appeared in *EVENT*, *The Fiddlehead*, *The Malahat Review*, *Parchment*, *PRISM International*, and *Stand Magazine* in the United Kingdom. Selections from *Surviving the Censor* were chosen as finalists for CBC Literary Awards in 2002 and 2005.

The poet wishes to thank the following organizations and cultural centres for their support: The Banff Centre for the Arts; the Ontario Arts Council for a "Works In Progress" grant and two Writer's Reserve grants; the Canadian Consulate, St. Petersburg, Russia, for the opportunity to deliver the Alexander Mackenzie Memorial Lecture of 2004; the Canada Council for the Arts; and The Artist's House, Herzeliya, Israel.

The publisher gratefully acknowledges the financial assistance of the Canada Council for the Arts and the Ontario Arts Council.

 Canada Council **Conseil des Arts**
for the Arts **du Canada**

ONTARIO ARTS COUNCIL
CONSEIL DES ARTS DE L'ONTARIO

Published in 2006 by
Seraphim Editions
238 Emerald St. N.
Hamilton, ON
Canada L8L 5K8

Library and Archives Canada Cataloguing in Publication

Aaron, Rafi, 1959–

    Surviving the censor : the unspoken words of Osip Mandelstam / Rafi Aaron ; editor, Allan Briesmaster.

Poems.

ISBN 0-9734588-7-9

    1. Mandelshtam, Osip, 1891–1938—Poetry. I. Briesmaster, Allan II. Title.

PS8551.A76S97 2006   C811'.54   C2006-900938-4

Editor: Allan Briesmaster
Cover photo: Gaye Jackson
Author's photo: Ruth Kaplan
Design: McNeill Design Arts

Printed and bound in Canada

To Eli

whose sensitivity and kindness
forever reminds me
that there is hope
for the future.

*

And to the spirit of
Osip Mandelstam

whose poetry took me on an odyssey
that went far beyond literature.

CONTENTS

I: AN INTRODUCTION TO OSIP MANDELSTAM

II: THE POET'S ARREST

III: EXILE

IV: ANOTHER SHADE OF DARKNESS— LIFE AFTER EXILE

VII: SURVIVING THE CENSOR

I

AN INTRODUCTION TO OSIP MANDELSTAM

I was born in the night of the second and the third
Of January in the eighteen ninety-first
Untrustworthy year, and the centuries
Surrounded me with fire.

—Osip Mandelstam, "Verses on the Unknown Soldier"

Let Us Begin at the End
(The Anonymous Voice from the Camps)

"delirious, starving, his chest caving in, he knew he was still alive"

his words fall
      silently like rain in the middle of the night, the world is asleep
or not listening

the words tap on the dark glass or the dream and are heard
      in the memory of a previous storm
                        they drop into tiny pools
that have not heard the news—no one is listening

and the poet goes on
      spilling words from a wound that is so perfectly round

and the words water the garden,
      skim the mountain and cleanse the newborn

some mistake this act for creation
          others call it art
          but it is the breath of the poet
singing and dancing
      and as long as his lips move
        and he can feel the words, the sharp words
the soft words and the words he will never use
        then he is alive

My First Meeting with Mandelstam
(Researcher's Notes #1)

His voice rose from somewhere, from a gorge or a
canyon, a lost year or a forgotten photograph. So soft, so
powerful, a whisper commanded me to follow him. And
so I travelled close to his words wearing the white sea
on my tongue. I reached the mountains or the coastal
plains, it made no difference, the night curled its lips
and spoke of darkness, and still waters dreamt of waves.
And in some faraway place I listened as laughter was
beheaded and buried behind the hilltops.

It was here along the open borders that I moved in and
out of his trance, a slave to a master I had never seen.
By the spring we crossed into the marshlands and I sank
into his words. And there on a moonless night old
women gathered without torches. The deep lines
running down their faces showed how close they had
sat to the fire. I turned away rubbing the ashes of his
burnt years over my eyes, listening as the silence was
sculpted with the thin edge of his verse.

Each line was a travel document: a passport, a ticket on
the tall ship and proof of my false identity. I went
further, opening a door, peering through a porthole of a
poem, a welcome guest and an intruder. When I closed
the book the earth shook and I heard the cry of the
underworld, a groan from the council of sages, and I
knew I could never return to the old ways of tending my
life.

The Word
(Osip)

What I expected from a word was magic. I wanted it to
flare up from the page: to dance in its own colours, say a
watered-down blue that could swim in the channel of
the ear or sun-burnt orange that would magnetize
moments out of lost memories. The word was to appear
and disappear, to be a reminder, a passing light, a
golden wand, a bell that stopped ringing that the reader
continued to hear. In the hermitage the word would
officiate over the silence stalking nuns and novices. The
word, and I mean the heavy word that had broken loose
from its form, fossilized with other meanings as it rolled
down the spine of a century, was to be a skipping stone
across time, a trusted guide who would lead you back to
the accident, the blood, the pale-faced mother and the
clean white sheets where the words were laid out. Later
you would say, "I have seen my birth in these words."

The words began to smoke from over the mountain and
across the streams. The smoke was sweet and pleasing,
an announcement, the pouch of the royal messenger,
stating that the poem would pass this way. Villagers
prepared sash cloth, orange peels and fire pits. These
were the first words. Like the first rains they carried
hope and the festival of water for the dying herd. Then
the clouds burst, a clap of thunder and there was
language, words pulling together, rowers on the long
barge paddling, propelling the magic into sound and
sight.

Now I was ready. I could hear them at the cave of my
mouth. Soon they would reach the light beyond my
tongue. My blood rushed and I ran through the town. I
felt the force of my own breath knocking on rooftops
kicking out shingles, saying over and over, "a poem is

coming through," and as the words turned inside me the hair on my arms rose and billowed. I was ready to fly over the horizon into verse, or migrate like this into prose. To remain calm I cradled myself in the fisherman's song my mother had sung to me. These were not the words I had prayed for in the final moments but still they might be a sailor's sign for a good catch, so I tossed out whatever I was holding. It should have sunk like an anchor but instead I heard the sound of fishnets slapping the water.

What Mandelstam Meant to Russians During the Stalin Years
(The Anonymous Voice from the Camps)

Wait for the night when the half moon swings in a hammock of purple fog and the stars are not sharp enough to cut their way through the black sky. Draw the curtains in the room, extinguish the oil lamps and fear lights up within you. Extend a hand like a white cane. The things you know so well are no longer familiar. The chair, the bed, the glass bowl breaks. The fish pursue the fleeing water (what choice do they have?) and receive the final lesson about life on earth. Alone by the window the eyes eventually adjust and you begin to live in darkness.

Now imagine that during this period the smallest of flames is somehow flickering outside your window. It has the strength of the morning sun breaking through your shutters. It is all that separates you from the darkness of the day and the darkness of the night. You spend your life by this flame and melt into its glow. After many hours days or months you believe you can train the flame to leap higher on the walls or to crawl under the desk. Real or imaginary, this flame is how you survive, cook your meals and read your government-approved books. Finally you cuddle up to the flame for companionship, take note of its beauty and changing shape.

Years later when light is restored, nothing is ever as bright. You are told of the burning blue jets of the meteor as they fire across a bow of sky and to shield your eyes during the eclipse. But you dismiss this, knowing the most powerful light can only be seen in total darkness.

Leaping Continents
(Researcher's Notes #2)

Somehow I am leaping continents. Writing in North America about Stalin's Russia, I survive the coldest winter and yet another purge. And last week the tanks rolled out of Lebanon and I moved, barefoot and open shirt, to my home along Israel's Northern border.

I am always tempted to describe the beauty of Shamir's surroundings. It is still a secret that I whisper to myself. And when I find a word I can trust I hide it in a cigar box or a drawer filled with buttons and bolts where it remains anonymous. And when I am starving for this place, for the sweet smell of the orchards at 4 p.m., for the voice of a single bird and the view of the valley swimming through dark brown, green and opium-red waters, I gather these words and carefully place them on my tongue.

Then there is Moshe Kagan and his watercolours. He keeps no secrets, holding the mountains and the valley perfectly still. He points to the coach house and transfer station where red is burning but not yet crimson. Where bright green parts from its family and is carried off by a yellow clan and there by the shaded blue shadows others mingle and wait to be tied to names. Over the fields untamed orange, its wild mane flying across the sky, inflames the pale blue clouds. And there is emptiness that is silence as he reveals those places where colours marry in the cotton fields or mountainsides under the green leaves and turned up earth.

He too leaps continents never forgetting how he survived living in the forests and fighting with the partisans. His drawings "of Stalin and his work" (as he calls them) make the viewer stop, turn, beg like a person who lived through these horrors for the end, but the paintings go on. He strangles what he loves most (remember the story of the family hiding, the house search and the child who cannot stop coughing; the mother suffocates her baby), he moves to charcoal, black and shades of black. Here there is no room for misinterpretation.

A Moment's Rest from My Life
(Osip)

Sometimes I want to lie down in the tall grass and stare up at the night sky and watch the poems that have moved off into the highest sphere as they shed their light or water the earth with hope. And like the young lovers who count the stars, I too want to believe in tomorrow. And if I lie here long enough the earthly burdens that weigh my body down will fall away and I will float with the ease of the clouds.

Understand this. I did not chart this course nor did I abandon it once it became clear. What happened happened quickly. After the revolution many things would be lost forever. I feared for the life of a single word: poisoned by the regime, I discovered it listless on the page.

During this time the muse was hibernating and my poems slept peacefully. Then there was crying and the muse would not be consoled. I wrote of the famine as I watched the truth starve. I became what I am, a witness, which is to say I entered old age in my youth.

But here with the night sky in the tall grass none of this matters. I could lie here and listen forever to the night wind as it strikes up its familiar tunes whistling through branches rippling the streams or running its long fingers through my hair. But time is loud and short. I hear each second break into segments as it separates from me. My hourglass houses stones. The seconds drop and smash into tiny pieces returning home as slate. The muse is aware of this and visits me frequently, knocking at my door saying, "Here write this down." And now it visits at all hours of the day and night and I have no time to lie in the tall grass, and the whistle in my ear is not the wind but my Master calling me home and I am happy to obey.

Mandelstam—A Biography
(Researcher's Notes #3)

Do not begin with a date of birth. Remember we are discussing the man who smashed the glass of the hall clock so that the hands stopped in 1938. Then the minute hand and the hour hand bent themselves into another form—a compass or a navigational instrument—so that his words sailed on to another century.

Now spread the years apart so that the facts fall free of the man as he strides to the podium, the poems opening like a room among the ruins, the light crawling out of the veins of rock and onto the altar, the artifacts and the large squares, those mysteries where you placed your thoughts and returned to watch them be blessed or beheaded by a power that propelled the darkness through the day.

Then remember his breath was a flame and a fountain, the secret police were tortured by what they could not catch or kill, the poems were free and stalking the country, the peasants harvesting nouns when there was no wheat.

Death. All we can say for certain is no one ever saw him dead, there is no grave or marker, the poet's words continued to work, mingling with the common language, hammering at the knee of an idol.

Second last sighting: January 1990. After fifty-two years of living in faded notebooks and whispers that circled through immigrant cafés his voice was officially heard in Moscow.

Last sighting: two nights ago. The streets were dark and deserted. The storm pounded my windows. I gripped the wheel and saw a man without an umbrella or a hat. His pace was unhurried and he did not delude himself by holding a jacket or a newspaper over his head. He did not stop or take notice of me. He just kept walking.

Translating Mandelstam
(Researcher's Notes #4)

It has nothing to do with language and everything to do
with the sudden breaking of glass, winter walking through
summer, the parade of exotic animals, colours I have
never seen and little fires that warm me here and there.

In the tranquil night air there is your voice in the desert,
a rebellion against the season, the assassin's bullet
knocking out the eye of a reader. But who can translate
the work of a man who reaches into darkness to spread
a finger of light and submerges his secrets into sounds?

Everywhere there is music. The Russian reader taps a
foot or finger, the village is decorated with silver
ornaments, the ice breaks and the festival of spring
begins. As the river flows there is the clash of
consonants, the tempo of the shepherd's staff and the
joyful play of nouns before the words arrive with a
message.

So much is lost (I could say), so much will never reach
the needy. I want to be the blind witness who
understands the tension in the reins, the bells on the
horse's harness and the fate of the old woman crossing
the street. Or to eavesdrop on the wind, hearing the
whispers and the two tiny drums the lovers beat.

I wander to the point where words end and sensations
take over: the hot blood charting veins crosses the
border of language. Then the fire of the forge flames, a
scream is heard, and words are cooled in the translator's
tears.

I turn back to enter Mandelstam's world
the gate closing behind me
is the only sound I understand.

II
THE POET'S ARREST

It is typical of regimes in which all power rains down from above and no criticism can rise from below, to weaken and confound people's capacity for judgement, to create a vast zone of grey consciences that stands between the great men of evil and the pure victims.

—Primo Levi, *Moments of Reprieve*

The Years of Silence
(Osip)

*"When the morphine from the revolution wore off the
surgeons from the secret police closed the wound. Small
needles pulled a thread through the country that sealed our
lips. Who could possibly possess the strength to toss out one
word of truth and not be crushed by it?"*

When the truth could no longer be transmitted we
stood and were silent.

The wind held its breath and joined us, the fruit rotting
on the trees and the ground. There were signs: wood
carvings, etchings, hieroglyphics and sometimes we
smuggled a wink or a frown to a friend but words met
their fate in the forests as they were tossed into the open
alphabet or severed without a sound from the meanings
that held them in this world. And they rose above the
village and the valley, bursting like a cloud that held
thunder and lightning in its belly.

And so we turned our backs on the muse as it begged
for the warmth of a reader's hands or the solitude of a
white page. And sometimes it happened in a cramped
room on a damp floor or in the tall grass the sun had
withered—a poem was born and quietly placed in the
ground where it might grow into and out of this century.

The years grew obese, devouring art, igniting the
silence, the explosions abandoning sound. When the
flashes of light died darkness inherited our words,

> and what could never be
> written or spoken
> weaved its way
> into the mind
> and echoed in the ear.

While I Wrote This a Battering Ram of Knives Excavated Old Wounds— The Poem Attacking Stalin
(Osip)

There is something deep inside me, I don't know who placed it there. Perhaps it entered me the way the north wind enters a woman's dress knocking loudly on her knees, making her head turn and her face flush before freezing the flesh of her thighs. Sometimes I think it sank into me when my birth water was washed away. It doesn't matter how it arrived. It's here and insists on going for long walks to take the night air.

Once and only once the days were little finger bells that sounded so nicely. Then the dancing stopped, the band shell collapsed, and now there is only the air playing single notes on a rasping lung. This does not matter to you, BUT (finally that word appears like a mountain cutting off the view of the valley I loved to look at) the hour hand has hypnotized your days and meaningless motions fill your life. And this thing inside me wants to waken you. It is as if the forests were on fire and the squirrels and earthworms adjourned their meetings and the wild flowers with no next of kin perished. Now people pretend that the pinks and the purples that coloured the hills never existed, maybe they saw something else. A white sheet at midnight can be mistaken for a ghost or so I have been told.

Pay attention to what I am about to say. What is deep inside me moves away from the darkness, the lily pads, the tiny fish and the coral reef where it breathes and bathes, multiplies and manipulates the light into red and yellow streamers. And just as it is blindfolded and the final commands are given, it speaks because it cannot be silenced the way a volcano sitting still for years suddenly shakes and pulls open its lower lip spilling knowledge over the world. (After this there are always tears, destroyed thoughts, uninhabitable ideologies and the smell of smoke reminds us that Truth is forever burning.)

And what bubbles from within me fills broken boxcars, becomes fruit in a petrified forest or finds its way to a dying river that lives on in the memory of spring, the smell of muck and weeds that once filled its empty belly.

The Writing of That Poem
(Nadezhda)

I knew the poem on Stalin was coming. For so long Osip was silent. But standing next to him I could feel the tremors running through his body. Heat rose off his head and darkness filled his eyes: the poems were rising within him. Soon they would erupt. This was a natural course and I never thought of stopping it any more than I would have attempted to stop the coming season. These poems would destroy our lives. But how could I blame him? When a mountain explodes it does not say "my lava will burn the village below." Years ago he took an oath, one hand on *The Divine Comedy* the other on a blank piece of paper. Arrest, interrogation and whatever followed were not his concern. And so we were villagers living under the volcano. We knew the power of his poetry, the strength of our straw huts.

Listening to the Elevator
(Nadezhda)

"We participated in this ritual of the new era. It was similar to waiting for a response from the oracle. We had all asked the question 'when will they come for us?' and the answer arrived after midnight."

It was after midnight
and the elevator was moving

The eyes of the icon curled inward
a jagged nail crossed a vein
a door trembled and the rooms
of the heart were full

We lay in our sweat
the king's cortege passed by
the singers passed by
and half-spoken prayers leaped
to their final resting place

I said the elevator was moving!
fairytales and battle plans passed by
a knife and a sword pursued
by a bullet ran by
and in the hallway
muffled cries, shrieks
and tears

We tasted the damp earth
and could not untangle the legs
arms and breasts
in that lifeless orgy
of the mass grave

The elevator was moving
cannibals hung their skins
out to dry, flowers bloomed
and history hobbled on
and all anyone remembered
was a thorn
in the eye of laughter

3-5 Furmanov Street
(Researcher's Notes #5)

A pilgrim I take off my shoes and walk up stairs that
have crumbled years ago. I kneel where I need to and
recite what I know. This place is filled with one-eyed
dogs, black magic and words that hibernate and
somehow rise on the coldest of nights to warm you.

It was here that the riverbeds were sucked dry, that the
wind coughed and spat out a tooth and some old
litanies and a childless mother walked by swaddling her
dreams. Then the storm arrived with its mallets,
hammering a sheet metal sky.

On the night of the 13th, they came for you. On the
night of the 13th dark clouds were busy stalking
shadows, straw men were stuffing scarecrows, and a
circle was drawn around the corpse of a city. On the
night of the 13th an unwed star touched the white
shoulder of the moon (or so it was recorded), four men
and one informer pried open the casket of fear; grey
hair, dead eyes and disease fell to the floor. The song
had begun, no one would mistake the melody.

Old friend, the incision is deep. They have struck the
heart, your poems are turning red. The emptiness fills
everything, it roams through this space and is larger
than the house where you once lived. The breeze from
the hill sits quietly on a log paying its respects, and a
song is played on a flute by someone who has never
heard happiness sing.

I wander down corridors that do not end. I journey on snowshoes over frozen fields until I reach the lilacs of spring. It is here where I set up my tent, here where nostalgia is performing a three-act play no one wants to remember.

And now to pretend that this place never existed; to destroy it, to abandon it, to erase it from the memory of brick and mortar, to bend it until it is bowed. And so they continue to bury a man who is already dead. But the ghost is not silent. He calls out his name and reads what he has written. The poems reverberate through the beams that were ploughed into the earth. The words are steel spikes entering the arm. I am proud to wear this pain.

Lubyanka
(The Anonymous Voice from the Camps)

I walk by your front door there is no one home.
The night is silent the leaves cautious as they move
down the street.

Lubyanka the century is shaking, every stone is
a tear, admit what you are: the half sister of truth,
the commissar of fear, and the poison the hungry
were fed.

I want people to know you are the four letters of
death, the chamber beneath the chamber, and a
word imprisoned in the mouth.

Yes this is the garden where summer was tortured,
where birch trees were stripped and the earth piled
high. Here we witnessed the suicide of the wind
flying into windows that never opened. After that
freedom confessed and the hours were led away.

Lubyanka—blue running for its life in a sea of red,
galvanized rain falling on the children, and a bullet
hole in the ankle of the dream.

And beyond the shadows where they work the fields
matching bone to bone, you are the prayer for the
dead tied to a whipping post that screams out as
another secret is exhumed.

Finally there is the story of the old man sailing out
of the front gate in a shoe, a fable perhaps, but
here how does one speak of reality?

The Line—Mandelstam's Suicide Attempt
(The Anonymous Voice from the Camps)

there was the constant tapping
the coughing that continued all night
and do not forget the faces
that were blurred but still visible
as he drew the line
over and over, chanting its silence
digging for something deeper
a word or a colour he had never seen

then the red chestnut and the red apple
passed before him, the bright red carriage
the song of red that would carry him away
with a voice and a violin and the breathless
smokestacks of industry
spinning out more and more red
that covered his arm

the line was beautiful and blushing
for all to see, the slight curves
the ruby lips and without a whisper
the imagination opened
like the young lovers' thighs

the line changed direction
hunting the great vein
set up traps and camped
in the stairwells of winter

do not believe all you have heard
the line wasn't straight
it angled off in places, broke in others
curved like a spine or the border
embanked by a river, trees and the thick foliage

smugglers love—it was a place where thousands
disappeared, a memory that continued to erupt, a fountain
without water

perhaps what he drew
was not a line
but a perfect circle
a brush stroke
a signature in time
a last look
a secret sign
or simply the closing of a book

Case No. 4108—Accused—Citizen Mandelstam, O.
(Researcher's Notes #6)

So this is what you have become—a number, a file in a black folder, a signed confession, a violet rose in the burial ground, a seed of sunset sprouting out of the sky that the day has already forgotten.

This is where migrating birds have their tail feathers plucked out, where the muse takes flight in its final moments, where laughter is skinned and nailed to the wall and momentary madness breeds more madness.

The cold stones offer few details. I searched for the bloodstains, the glacial cap that falls from the eye as it goes dim, and the almost snoring sound an unconscious man makes as he's dragged across the floor.

(Do not crave more facts hoping for something better, say a lesser form of evil. This is all we know: people travelled far, to the Baltic sea to the Karelian forest and other deserted spaces where the air had never met a smokestack, fire or forge and still they could not cleanse their nostrils from the smell of the crematoriums.)

Here you are the doomed traveler who spends his days searching for a way out of a parable. Later things will change, your body will disappear but your poems will not. You will become the excuse that goes sour on the tongue of party officials before it ever ripens into something believable, a poster scraped from a wall that remains fixed in the memory of children: the man fighting a lion who wrestles his way into dreams, with your fierce eyes and outlawed hand.

There is no way home dear poet, the forest has grown around you and the voice of the child screaming inside you for his mother is that of a boy who has fallen into a well, a strange echo one hears only when drinking water.

Yes, time is ticking out loud. Saddle the muse to the fastest horses, pray that your avalanche of words will cover everything, even your own grave.

Nikolai Bukharin
(Researcher's Notes #7)

There must have been shouting from deep within him,
restless hours where he chased sleep through empty
nights, and eyes that could see through the steel doors
of doctrine and onto the faces of those who were
sentenced to death. The Moscow river froze in the
winter and flowed in spring and so it was with
Bukharin, his blood encountered those small ice
breakers, the abandoned orphan or the taste of poverty
that kept sticking to his tongue, and from the heights of
the Politburo he pronounced it summer, stole a tree or
smuggled an orchard into his world, violets and
daffodils popped out of buttonholes all so he could
burn in a pyre of summer, the sun setting him free. He
reached out to save Mandelstam with the song of the
drowning man which filled his lungs and he knew by
the time he arrived at the chorus he would no longer be
a member of the ruling party, only a man who
encountered his conscience behind an unlocked door.

The Naming of the Miracle
(Nadezhda)

Even when we pronounce the word miracle it drops off the tongue anchoring us to an event, it resurrects the days of prophets pilgrims and plagues. Later it travels through the night on a caravan of words that crosses the blistered lips of men and women who eat and drink from the cracked bowl of time and all they can feel in their throats is that moment when the fortress of their understanding fell and flamed and their eyes glowed.

Every miracle has a name. It travels dirt roads and sandy plains carrying the equator in its side pocket and an ocean or two on its back and when it stands before you on stilts everyone knows its name.

And so Exile arrived and I followed this vision through the darkness until dawn drifted out of my eyes, and somewhere in the clearing where woodcutters worked the jaws of the earth opened and my husband's voice rose from Moscow's wounded soil.

From the offspring of evil I had expected to hear the silence that cannot be punctured as it stretches out over the years while a single question floats like a drowning man to the top of my thoughts—dead or alive?

But all I heard was the hammer against the anvil, the pounding of the Name onto silver strands for bracelets and bands that would circle my days with light.

Yes Exile was a miracle and those who heard about it looked heavenward. I danced it around my mouth and held it on my tongue for as long as I could, then I swallowed this biblical remedy and fell from the weight of its wonders without ever thinking that in a country like Russia one miracle would never be enough to save my husband.

III

EXILE

And the vilest: we
were the public that applauded or yawned in its seats.
The guilt that knows no guilt,
                        innocence
was the greatest guilt.

—Octavio Paz, "San Ildefonso Nocturne"

Voronezh
(Nadezhda)

The darkness drops its anchor on our lungs and we
feel the weight of each breath. Here even the wind
is helpless as it breaks its back on our windows
and moans outside our door. I have ransomed my
memories from Moscow and soon I will be free
but the war goes on and they continue the assault
on the weakened walls, the burned-out interior, the
holy of holies where our thoughts are stored and
once again I am defenseless.

Listen: the footsteps, the voices, the ones that
speak for darkness and the ones that speak from
death, repeating their words, their warnings. There
is nowhere to retreat, the country is on fire and
people swim through the flames with fluorescent
arms,

Oh Voronezh!

dark and damp you entered the south side of my
bones, creaking, opening the hinges that shivered
in my blood you sank your sonorous songs into my
soul. Your bleak sky is a fortune I have already
foretold, and I know this winter will never
surrender the earth, no it will hold on, cradling the
snow in frozen fists until its lips are blue and
motionless.

Voronezh you are buried under glass, in a facade
of work and your habitual practice that leaves
boulders in the way of the blind. Here everything
has turned into a mystery, the old man playing the
balalaika without strings, the seasons marooned on
a calendar, and always the axe of the executioner
above our heads. Voronezh is this life or death?

And now I want to clear my throat and speak but soon my mouth will be full of sand so I leave this to the archaeologists who will dig up the facts one bone at a time.

Voronezh I am calling to you across the years of exile over ramshackle houses and a railway line that leads back to civilization and through the winters that never forget how cold life can be, and somewhere out there on one of your hills the sun was pinned at the point of the interrogator's question, then the light sank into the snow and that is all, that is all.

"My Greatest Creative Period Was in Exile"
(Osip)

When the prison gates opened I did not believe
Stalin would let me walk into exile.

My death would be slow and silent, the bullet
would turn the colours of the seasons as it passed
through my life, ending in the winter that was
never white, the frozen branches would shiver and
shake as all witnesses do.

At every turn I waited for them to clasp my arms
and pin my poems behind my back, but they
granted me another hour to organize my words
into bold formations.

And in those days and in those nights I wrote like a
man who must convey all his knowledge by dawn.
I entered the years I would never see, reaching for
the fruit that would ripen on the reader's tongue.

In the fields where all borders end I grew into my
grandfathers' wisdom, bending with the weight of
what I carried, and as the hours pinned me to the
earth I searched for a breath and my heart beat the
irregular beat of a drummer who no longer counts
time.

Living My Death
(Osip)

*"After his release from prison he was so close to the
grave, the smell of damp earth was in his hair, the
darkness in his eyes and the smallest of worms
transporting mud over his body."*

When they did not place me in front of a firing squad my
life ended.

They shackled me to the moment of death and I dragged it
through days and dreams.

Later I severed myself from the world sitting in the hollow
of a poem waiting for a vision to appear.

When I emerged from the shadows my eyes were clear,
my hand steady on the page. I headed for the light

> but the moment had grown
> into a large stone
> and there I was
> dragging a marker for my grave
> over the earth.

The Recurring Dream
(Nadezhda)

The gates of the prison parted and Osip appeared. Somehow
my husband had survived the winter returning to rest on my
shoulder and I fed him from an open hand. At first I thought it
was a dream, a Russian dream, where a woman is reunited
with her lover who has been taken away, but his voice called
to me and I knew he was alive. I clutched him, not physically,
but his presence and his words and every moment welded to
our names. And we walked away, as if walking out of a
photograph, his eyes retelling the tale of our first days. I
wanted to speak, to ask questions, but the moment would not
move on. We were together. Then a treasured wind touched
my cheek, the cloak of a horseman and the sheath of the
hunter passed by. I stuffed the ribbon from this gift into my
pockets, knowing it was more than a keepsake.

A Poem in Praise of Stalin—
How I Tried To Save My Wife
(Osip)

The Ode summoned me on a morning when
nothing else would do, when death, that visitor
who had overstayed his welcome, said goodbye
and packed my bags. I moved towards him slowly,
the way a lion tamer approaches the unfamiliar.
With my hands trembling I poured out the lexicon
of the Russian language. This was all I owned, this
was all they wanted.

Do not judge me! The Ode was for the day after they
took me away and I was only a whisper among my
poems, only a name approaching greatness, a figure
made out of snow that would one day melt into
words.

I became a hunter trapping animals I loved. And so
I released them in places where they would never
be captured in verse again. You see I wanted to carry
the coffins of the poor to that place behind the hill,
to wave the matador's cape so the dictator would
see red and to explore the left hand by ignoring the
right. But mostly I wanted to retell the story of the
boy who jumped off the cliff. The villagers say he
flapped his arms and those tiny hairs billowed like
feathers and when he crashed on the rocks his nose
resembled a beak, his tiny neck belonged to a
sparrow. Perhaps he was pushed, or so I thought, as
I wrote the Ode. Later I wondered how I would look
when I was dead among my words and old age had
passed me by without even closing the door on a
room full of memories.

Anna and Osip
(Nadezhda)

*"Whoever portrays the Kremlin Mountaineer will
enslave a generation of words."*

Now a sound broke out over the city stumbling
from one house to the next. It lingered in the air,
attached itself to columns, branded the tower and
anchored the wind to a southern port. I tell you the
clocks did not strike that night, as the fiefdoms of
silence united so that insects could eavesdrop on
two poets as they spoke for the last time.

Do not look away when I say their voices rose over
red trees and mountains and above the indigenous
cries of orphans searching for a way home. From
this hill they reunited the lost tribes of their faith
and fed the muse. They went on, sharpening
words, exploding a verb, calibrating the silence.

Soon it would all collapse and amid the decaying
facts and the molested dreams there would be
poems to nourish the newborn, poems to suffocate
the sorrow, and poems that would barter the day
for the night and the night for a single soul that had
been left hanging without a husband or a son.

IV

ANOTHER SHADE OF DARKNESS— LIFE AFTER EXILE

"Let me finish my work"

—Isaac Babel, in his final plea to the Russian authorities

After Exile
(Osip)

"So this was my punishment, to be a wet nurse for a stillborn freedom."

And so we returned to the promise that was never given, returned with our hands in shackles and our pockets filled with poems.

We sifted through the language of hunger devouring the words, bread, and cabbage, shuffling our feet in long lines and around clerks who remained motionless.

Wherever we walked we searched for a grave: as someone said, "You entered the desert searching for sand."

Then the silence came and we were invalids unable to move in the world. The hours wasted away. We waited for a knock on the door, for my heart to stop or insanity to sully my verse.

Every night we heard the pounding of nails. They were building our future. And like all condemned people we witnessed the construction of our death.

Facing Another Day
(Osip)

I began again with the strength of the great men in
the Moscow Circus pushing myself off a mattress
and into another day. On the smallest vessel that
sailed I imported foreign thoughts that had been
polished along the coast. When the cargo arrived I
sat with a shrunken head and leaves that smoked
the memory and filled the air with the aroma of
Armenia. I bandaged the hours from bleeding away,
I turned to the north and the south, turned on a
weakened body and a frail heart and watched the
words as they ran out of my mouth, tripped over
stones, were stranded or strapped to the long oar,
waiting for the boatman who would never arrive.

I Am Tired
(Osip)

I am tired of the burlesque show of clouds that reveals
nothing but sky and I am tired of the harmless poems. I
want words that devour a limb or the steel leg of theology,
words that ignite the haystack, burn the village and
blacken the bells. I am tired of the poets who cannot sing,
who strangle the muse with the stem of a rose. But mostly
I am tired of looking into the orphans' eyes, tired of the
nights that vanished and the girls that rise like the sun
from the bushes and street corners, tired of my ghosts
walking beside me, tired of this blindfold. Shoot already!
Shoot! But all I hear is the grieving family that is a chorus
for the wind. Look over here, behind the tree, in that field
or under that rock for the true voices of this country.
Forget what you have heard. My poems are the days
pacing up and down the stone steps of your cell, the
scream forever trapped inside your ear and the scar
without the history of a wound. But more then anything I
am the colour in the left hand corner of the tapestry, say
autumn green, that bleeds over the sun, the swans and
the paddleboats, so that you mourn this scene. I am not
asking for much. I want the alchemist instead of the
watchmaker, a captain without a compass and someone
who can levitate words without dimming the lights.
Understand I am tired and the state will not forgive me,
but the children will remember how I made strange
noises as the procession passed by and that I was the
rotting breath that blew out the candles behind the icon. I
can no longer listen to the moaning from the
convalescing poems as they are wheeled in their beds
from one victory to another. I am tired but before I go I
want to hear one verse that will scratch the eyes, inflame
the skin and make the strongmen of this nation shake. I
want to see them bite down hard on the truth (the way
the old shopkeepers tested a gold piece) and taste fear.

The Market in Leningrad
(Nadezhda)

"The end came one day when we met two acquaintances,
who did not avert their eyes, as people should when
encountering a convicted person, but looked through
us, as if we had never existed."

It was in the market in Leningrad that we began to
understand our fate. There in that lonely place where
the dark sky was nailed to the ground, the instruments
of faith shattered and dead promises lay in the street.
Under the red sign the drunken rains fell on us, fists
pounding on metal sheds and shutters, and the night
swallowed another star.

Do not come closer, do not approach this place, now or
ever, it is not the water but the wave, the unforgiving
meridian green that circles the lungs with the aftertaste
of life: stale air, washed up magnolias and the coarse
salt that preserves a final thought.

And now to retell the tale the way my ancestors did,
leaving signs and footprints in the hard clay for others
to ponder. Do not expect answers, only fragments
scratching the eye, only the severed head of darkness
bleeding through your dreams, the cannibal's teeth and
the flaying of the flesh off an idol (that's what happened
to our living gods). Further on a list of names, foreign
and forgotten, and finally all that intrudes into your
world is the cheekbone of a child.

There in the market in Leningrad the mystery ended as
we watched the people carving our faces off
photographs, removing us from memory, and all the
while the shovel digging into the earth, the sound of
good citizens burying the Mandelstam name before
Stalin could dispose of our bodies.

This Light
(Osip)

This light has deserted me. It rested in my bones, accompanied my blood on its journey through the dark waters, the thin island arteries where it danced barefoot by the fire. I heard a voice then I heard the choir. The light was singing its song, dressed in the yellow feathers of the sun, spreading a message of warmth. And the sound of light crackled in the burned out nights, it rained on the windows of a dark continent and bled its gold into dreams. But the black magic grew and swallowed the sword and the flame. And I cried out for one ray of light that would blind me so that I could stroll my fingers over words and see the world that I knew.

Osip's Second Arrest
(Nadezhda)

I screamed without opening my lips, a scream
filling mineshafts and tunnels and melancholy
orchards ploughed under the earth, and I entered
the smallest of rooms seeking that broken moment,
that shriveled memory that whispers from the
shallow graves where mothers come to mourn
their children.

Hear me when I say I woke from this dream to
watch the boat with my husband drifting away. I
wanted to shout out but where were my words,
they too had been dragged off. And I wanted to
move but the crossbeams and collapsed years of
our lives lay on my limbs. It was here they left
me to die. But I remembered my husband
creating, moving his lips, inviting the air to play
on his tongue. And with all my strength I pried
open my mouth and took a breath. Then I
collaborated with the night moving permanently
into my shadow, hurling the remaining hours of
my life into Osip's work, proclaiming his season.

And so I turned to face winter, barefoot, starving
and still carrying these poems, with all their
weight, as if I were carrying my husband back to
the people, back to Mother Russia.

V

HOPE ABANDONED

That's when the ones who smiled
Were the dead, glad to be at rest.

—Anna Akhmatova, "Requiem"

An Open Letter to the Unacknowledged One
(The Anonymous Voice from the Camps)

There was no prayer in the camps. Hope and belief had been scorched out of every man long ago. It was so obvious it stuck out like the bones that protruded from the faces of prisoners as they waited for their time to expire, for a finger to be pointed, and for their bodies to fall. The end was so close but we were carried away on a caravan of days and it seemed as if we would live forever. During this period a new form of petitioning the Unacknowledged One was created. Those who were too weak to recite their request did so by urinating into the frozen snow. They left one line to represent a stick man and a second line crossing it out.

we are the drowning men
who have never spoken your name
our lives ended long ago
when we were pulled from our homes
our bodies have been slow in receiving the message
they fight on without knowing

we are waiting in these camps
for death to arrive
we have no fears
except that we may survive
to meet another day another memory
if you are the Ruler the Power and the Source of Mercy
please, please, take us now

even in this dark place
we have never acknowledged you
or lit a clump of wax
to illuminate your name
our voices are strange to your ear
but this is not a prayer but a plea
from men who have reached the bottom
and continue to drown

The Prayer of the Believers
(The Anonymous Voice from the Camps)

But there were those who believed. Through chattering teeth
they sang songs of praise to the L-rd and watched their words
ascend to the heavens on a cold breath. They thanked the
Eternal One (as they called him) for all the gifts he had bestowed
upon them. "We did not question him in times of prosperity and
so we will not abandon him in this difficult hour. We remain his
devoted subjects, loyal foot soldiers following the Almighty's
plan on earth. The body is the shell that crumbles. We work and
work to save our souls. So let us sing," they said, and they joined
hands and sang: "Our faith is the vessel of the L-rd, it is
unsinkable and sails the storm as it does the calm sea."

G-d, Creator and Ruler of the universe
we offer you praise and thanks for this day
which you have granted us
we turn our faces to your light
our prayers to your ears

O Great and Mighty One
part these dark days
so that we may see the sun
as we work these fields
in the final moments of our lives

Strengthen us, reward us
place us in the house of the L-rd
where time is unmeasured
and eternity the reward
of the righteous

Grant blessings to our loved ones
spare them reunite them
so they may sit at the table
and bless your name
and speak your greatness
provide for them dear L-rd
provide for them

This Is Not a Letter
(Osip)

Date: Unknown

Second River Transit Camp (near Vladivostok)
Soviet Far East

This is not a letter.

It is a warning to the birds that circle this camp, a
message in a cracked bottle that slits the hand of
those who reach for it, so that we may all taste our
own blood. This is not a letter or a promise I forgot
to fulfill, only a funnel of smoke rising off the
plains. People look and can't believe what they see.
The world has foundered. Whatever I say you
already know. But I remember the sounds of
laughter when they placed it in the icy waters to see
if it would drown or freeze first, and that morning
they slaughtered the cherry blossoms and they fell
on the fresh snow as teardrops of blood: how
beautiful they lay there as if on a white canvas and I
stared at them saying: "this is the work of
professionals."

Do not deceive yourself, this is not even a message
but a tribal rite we invented here on the last outpost
of earth, where dysentery has purged us of all
beliefs. Others suck on a cigarette stub blowing
smoke through the narrow lanes of memory, I
command words to follow me. Remember this is
not a letter. It is madness in the last moments, the
seat closest to the podium where the poet swallows
the shards of a language he once spoke and
somehow they become lodged in your throat. This
magic is called the muse.

If this was a letter what would I say? That the sword repeatedly plunged into my childhood, that the castle walls were made of paper and that there are fifteen stages of starvation. What other explanations do you need? Surrender? It is no longer possible. The advancing armies have retreated to their mistresses, medals and boot makers. There is no one to surrender to (and what's worse, the bullet with my name on it was swallowed by a starving man). No, I wasn't surprised that evil grew into a giant or that the party calls these pyramids of bone art.

I tell you this is not a letter but the charred remains of a man, the self, exposed on the banks of a nameless river once named after me. It is the words performing a final ceremony, the privilege of priests, it is the tarnished bugle playing stiff notes, and it is the remainder of love scattered through the house and sorrow festering in the sheets.

I have to go now. I cannot send this to you but that does not matter. I will write again soon. If you can, send food, money, and warm clothes.

Osip Mandelstam

P. S. Mostly food, I have discovered a plot to poison me and cannot eat the food they are giving me.

Examining Mandelstam's Life Through One Spring Day in 1928
(Researcher's Notes #8)

*"When the show trial was announced we interpreted
this as a death sentence. We bowed our heads and
swallowed our words, allowing them to enter the
kingdom of silence."*

And now to recall the day as overcast or sunny, the story
retelling itself with different names, the spear of a word
and the net that entangled so many by his side

> and the seasons circled around him
> and his words circled through
> the borders that men make
> crawling to the tip of the tongue
>
> he looked at the stagnant waters
> the petrified forest that said nothing
> and noted the arthritic branches
> curved like the fingers of justice
>
> then he entered the singular
> the unholy

and when he spoke
his voice was the scream
of volcanic ash on a river of red dust
and the rumour twisted
into tiny threads
that tickled the ear
it was old news, the recital of how the world began
with G-d's long fingers strumming the trees
and some say it was a chariot of fire
an unclaimed victory
or the peculiar sound
of one man speaking

Mountains remained mountains, a dictator held his throne but something changed, a whisper leaked into the silence, the river returned emptying its pockets of silt on the shore, and the chains that bound the lips and limbs of a country broke ...

And five elderly men returned to their homes. Five flames danced in the eyes of the women who were no longer widows. Darkness grieved, and joy spread quietly the way it does in a regime, without laughter or a smile, just the eyes illuminating the dark waters of the well, just the claw of the memory casting a shadow over the moment.

The Journey
(Osip)

The evening stars wander the plains, the stones speak
not of wind but of time. It is good for me to listen, to
chart the voices over the years, to remember the places
where I camped in the canyons with the poets who have
come and gone before me, where we baked our bread
and broke our verse, where we tracked shapes and
shadows onto a white coast that ran the length of a
page. And to recall how I skipped a noun through a
verse, with a strong hand and an arrogant smile.

But now I touch the earth and as I do I extend out of the
land like a tree that will serve the small fires of time, and
the old men who would walk through a century bearded
and barefoot on the white of a flame. One last time I
would break the mould or crack the ridge of language,
burning the waters, the fields of forgotten letters that
singe the reader's eyes.

And now to float on the water like a flightless bird who
waits to greet a foreign shore. Here the night and day
will always be cast in concrete hours. But there across
the sea time will appear as the head of a salamander. I
will follow it into the darkest blue and below to the grey
that is weak and white where the tip of the mountain
fills my mouth, and the news will spread that the lost
city is made of bone and blood that was shed on the
gates of knowledge.

There I will stand surrounded by the words I have
claimed as my own, and wait for the poems the world
will never hear, the ones that will harden on my tongue.

Sometimes
(Osip)

Sometimes in the night I am reminded of things that happened long ago. I recall how I took all the colours of my imagination and covered over the site that had cursed my eyes. And for that moment I was a painter not a poet who camouflaged this scene with the happiest of memories: our first family outings, the opening of the Summer Gardens and the sun shining off the silver helmets of the Royal Guard as we passed by. But now a limb punctures the canvas, a hand lies limp on my pillow, later a face turned sideways, teeth clamped on the last words, and always I am stepping over the bodies that have fallen off a cart and remain lying on the street.

Final Thoughts
(Osip)

The gates were closing early on this century and I was
determined to step inside or place my poems through
the iron rails. Night was a curious creature, its nocturnal
light filtered through green weeds and water shone on
my face. My body ached as I thought of the places I had
travelled. I could have betrayed my art during the
famine allowing it to starve but I was always stashing a
stale piece of ideology under my jacket. And I could
have betrayed myself looking the other way, stepping to
the side, or crawling through a tunnel where I buried
my thoughts—but I was never capable of learning any
language other than the one I spoke. Too many people
were walking bent over looking for their voices, lips
moving without even a whisper. And I was there the
moment the light fractured and splintered, not through
the eye, but through an invisible and unknown window.
I could see clearly and was sure of what I saw. In a
smokehouse out back I stored my words. This is what
the people craved. This is what Stalin feared. (I
remember the sunset. It is a postcard stapled on the
backboard of my mind, the way the red sky turned its
torch sideways burning the waves before bathing in the
amber waters). Time! It means nothing to me. I have
cheated it and smiled as I smuggled my future in writing
over its unguarded coast. I pretended never to be in a
hurry (that was my secret). I would stop to look in shop
windows as Time moved on to destroy others with the
words "soon" and "any day now" which were written in
blood and left to dry on door posts. Now the winter
seems like a backdrop for the Mariinsky Theatre and a
strange melody is sticking to my tongue. I don't want to
say goodbye. But fate has marked me and I stand here
facing the archers and a quiver of motionless days.

I Would (If I Had One More Night with You)
(Osip)

I would want you to hear the voice of starlight and
the moonless choir, the weeping willows and the
ferns straightening themselves into strings. I would
have led you to a forest and gathered these sounds,
encircled them with faded stars that I would polish
for you the way the elderly gentleman on Debinsky
Street used to shine his medals, with a loving hand
and focused eyes that never betrayed the battles he
had fought.

We would have walked to a clearing and stood ten
paces apart so I could watch your small hands
perform their everyday magic. And as the sky closed
in on us I would have removed the white linen from
the family chest, waving it like a flag, surrendering
the moments of my life without you.

I would if I had one more night with you watch the
spectators rise to their feet as I entered the arena to
face my fate, and there I would burn like the final
hours of summer, heroically throwing the last lance
of light precisely at the spot where darkness entered
your eyes. And then I would seal the wound that
watered the earth, cauterise our time with the fire of
a language I was learning to speak and a kiss that
had gone astray.

I would if I had one more night with you slander the
season for all its beauty and warmth, swim in my
own tears, scuttle our memories so they'd drown
before my death, so the weight of my name would
no longer bear down on your days.

VI

FALLING

Take me into the night where the Yenisey flows
And the pine-tree reaches the stars,
Because my blood is not wolf's blood
And only my equal shall kill me.

—Osip Mandelstam, Poem 227

Falling
(Osip)

I was falling
         backwards
                 into soft clouds
                        and empty years
falling
    as only I could fall
                with a whip and a prayer
      over untamed memories
                falling

*

until I was the black eye of the night and the puffed
eyelid that held the sky open for the dawn and then I
was the sound of a word awaking from dreaming
tongues on the rock face of a cliff speaking in a
voice that carried the wind

*

I fell
    like a snake charmer
               poisoned by something I said

I fell
    as all good men fall
              holding on to what made them
good

I fell
    as a shepherd falls
               over a mountain path (an
          occurrence that happens only once)

I fell
    like the most delicate creation, fluttering,
      spinning through light,
             as if
I had practiced this falling

          *

I heard the rattle of keys and sounds that were chained
to the ear for centuries slipping away, the meat cleaver
landed softly, the swan's wing thrashed water into
waves, and when the sky opened lightning curled
out of a cloud eluding thunder forever

          *

I fell
    and
        I fell
          like the years
               that never stop falling

          like the hangman
               suspended in my dreams
          feet tapping
               for a piece of ground

          *

all that separated me from this world was a concrete veil,
the wings of a seagull searching for a body and the story
of soft flesh

*

I fell
    so I would never have to fall
                                 again

I fell
    until I was the sound of falling

*

and I fell with the weight of my knowledge, the
force of a glacial hammer pounding out a continent
where I would live, the wind wrapped me in a
summer breeze (a fashionable shroud), I was turning
into a poem, a memorable song, a dirge, or the
memory of a dead man

*

I fell
    with the great light fractured wounded and white

             I fell
               like a mirage after the tongue
             tastes the desert

I fell
    like the elderly sun before evening
        and before the family of stars could arrive

    I fell
      out of the sky
    black and terrifying
    as if I would bolt into lightning
    or point an electric finger
    at my accusers
        a man without a body

and so I fell
    out of my name

*

the night poured itself into twilight, the blue scales
and the orange tail of the sun splashed frantically
in their final moments, a warm wind rose to confront
the season and a face that was no longer mine and the
candle that would have burned for years, and darkness
spilled over the brim of the earth

I called out to hear my voice one last time but it had
already fallen through me, the view was beautiful
but I did not spear it with a poem as I was no longer
a hunter preying on images, the tall grass waved as
if to say goodbye

*

The curtain opened
                    and I fell
                              through the stains
that covered my country
                    and the names of those

who had yet to be named

                              the winter winds
touched my cheek
                    the carnival was over

the wheel stopped
                    and I fell
                              through the cold creek
of my veins
               and I froze
                    and I fell
                              to a place I cannot describe

because I fell
               through my words
                              and as a poet
this is how I knew
               I had come to the end
                              of
                                    my
                                          fall

VII

SURVIVING THE CENSOR

*But in books much loved, and in children's games I
shall rise from the dead to say the sun is shining.*

—Osip Mandelstam, Poem 341

*And we will preserve you, Russian speech.
Mighty Russian word!
We will transmit you to our grandchildren,
Free and pure and rescued from captivity
Forever!*

—Anna Akhmatova, "The Wind of War"

When Manuscripts Burned
(The Anonymous Voice from the Camps)

*"The manuscript fought, kicking out the teeth of the first
flames, breaking the red fist and strangling the smoke. Then
the fire surrounded the words. We listened to the screams as
the skin peeled off the poems. We turned our heads unable
to watch our children burn."*

When manuscripts burned the world was on fire.
The ashes of poems fell as snowflakes. Black
became white and people stuck out their tongues to
taste their youth.

The poet walked into the flames reciting the word
"rain." The dying verses were carried away and
buried deep in the memory where the loom of the
weaver, opening and closing, pulled them into a
new fabric.

Another shortage was coming. Poetry was hoarded
and hidden in our bellies. It entered the narrow
hallways of the bones, where the marrow sipped
wine, danced and reclined.

Here the story stops but only to rest like an
epidemic entering a house through an open
window. It decides to kiss the cheeks of children
and fear becomes the mistress who embraces the
family in the stairwell or on the cold sheets as
they shiver.

In the evening there was calm. The stars (and there
is always mention of the stars) slept under a thick
blanket. Old men propped up their tired stories and
only their eyes told a different tale. Silently our lips
moved and poems were walking a tightrope above
the town; performers, yes, but also witnesses who
would one day speak for themselves.

The Woman Walking
(Researcher's Notes #9)

she is the woman walking out of the river
with two buckets of water
on a cedar pole across her shoulders
she is walking up the hill to a neighbouring village
she is not young
she is not grimacing
only the pole bends under the weight
of the pails, only the midday sun
refuses to cast her shadow,
only the children run by her,
this is Mandelstam's wife
carrying his poems through the world
barefoot on thorns and stones
careful not to spill a word
knowing if she does it will be gone forever
knowing that where every drop lands
a flower will blossom
                    out of season

Hiding Manuscripts
(The Anonymous Voice from the Camps)

*"Even the children understood: literature was a
dangerous game the family played."*

"Words were worth dying for." I reread that line.
The door opens and people are walking through
fear.

They hum secrets to themselves, mend their socks
and boil water.

On the table sits the forbidden fruit, everyone has
tasted it, everyone has been strengthened by it.

In a corner of the communal flat a man speaks to
himself, "The land is barren without literature."
Then he stares at his family.

Here there is a sacred pact between a father and his
daughter, similar to the nocturnal vows of the waves
to the moon. Nothing will ever be spoken and it
would be foolish to name the force that brings them
together.

I tell you there are incisions, internal pockets, places
where poems are hidden and bound to the blood.

In these rooms they kept Mandelstam alive, feeding
his words to the open ear and by removing the skin
of the wound, showing the world how science and
literature evolved.

Longevity
(Osip)

When they separated me from my body I sailed on swift streams and the backs of salamanders and sea urchins across the years and into the arms of the reader. I did not dream that my words would live forever. I permitted the reader to march triumphantly through the archways, to feel how others felt as they returned from my poems on peg legs to screaming crowds and streamers. As they waved and smiled the strength returned to my hands and I uprooted the poems and words fell like pillars and a cloud of dust rose. This was my breath. And like the bombed-out epitaph the poems remained standing in people's minds. They became marks on a map, a pond where people fished for their youth. Here among the rubble I let the readers touch me, stand on me and view literature from the precipice. In the dry season they brushed my words with fine combs and scooped handfuls of poems, sifting them through strained eyes and when they looked up from their dinner tables, prison cells and podiums to ask "what time is it" I answered with the accuracy of the bells in the clock tower. Now the mystery blossoms on their fingertips as they touch the page. Who will say I am not alive, that my words are not living, that my breath is not breathing when a reader looks at me and I speak? They will search for keys, trap doors and hidden passageways that would lead to a voice that speaks without a mouth. All they will find are words melted into giant hooks, question marks that pry at the locked treasures of church and state.

Natasha Shtempel and the
Evacuation of Voronezh
(Researcher's Notes #10)

She is there in the moonlight and the grey light that
accompanies the cold on its rounds of winter,
between the blades of the censor, fashioning history
into a season, there amid collapsing roofs and the
calloused lips of lovers.

She is there as the bombs drop between the secrets
of the city and the canopies of gold, and as a village
crumbles into proverbs. There to watch the slaving
nouns working the fallow fields, and the heated
discussion between the anvil and the ash.

Amid the lavender and the green, the capsized
memory and the fables that nibble at the corner of
history, she is there waving a fist full of poems, at
the very moment summer will surrender its red
sleeve to fall.

His Last Public Reading
(Nadezhda)

When he broke the silence his voice was the wind racing over
rooftops to rob the trees of their red apples or the hurricane
riding a window into a whirl over the city. And the words were
towers (everyone looked up), teams of horses pulling the reader
through the deepest part of a stanza and it was the moment
before sunrise when the light scratches the sky with one long
fingernail, it was crimson and it was orange, it was silver
dangling off an ear and charcoal performing black magic.

Friends, believe me when I say he was the messenger, the
malignant rumour spreading through our history. His voice was
the grappling hooks the sun saves for mountains and the chain
pulling us out of a shallow grave.

Here I wandered; here I bent down on one knee to rejuvenate
what had fallen. I could no longer see the walls or the
watchtowers; his voice was the birch, the sycamore and the pine
tree planting themselves in front of me.

Under the dim lights he recited what he knew. These were not
blessings or superstitions soaked in tears. No! This was the
tapping of the gavel in the high court where one word was tried
for treason, then another and another.

His voice became the song a condemned man never sings and
the laughter that floats on evil,
                                        the unforgiving biblical passage
that casts stones, shadows and sharpened prophecies into the
eyes of readers.

We were watching his words rise. We waited for the moment he
would leave us.

      Then his voice would be the unopened letter
      you would read one day.

The Noise of the Century
(The Anonymous Voice from the Camps)

He was the striking of a match: in darkness everyone
hears the light, the unfamiliar, the almost silent, the
squeaking pulleys raising the wind over the trees.

He was the incision in the clouds that does not shed
tears. No! No! What am I saying, he was the fist of
the night assaulting the city, a steel finger in the eye
of the Kremlin.

Some have said he was the sound of danger
approaching on its wooden leg and backdoors bolting
or the snapping of a twig in the forest of fears.

But I know this—he was the silence the day after the
disaster, telling a story without a word. He stood
over there, beyond the walls of language, a name no
one would say, the registered physician at the birth
of rebellion.

Outside my window he was the beak of winter, the
knock on the door, the fist of the Cheka pounding on
the brain of every citizen.

Then he was the sound of the slaughter and the
sacred words a poet elongates with his last breath.

Later we all agreed he resonated in the items left
behind: an empty cup, a torn jacket and an old book.

Walking with Mandelstam
(Researcher's Notes #11)

Once I thought that if I walked with you to the end
of Russian literature, bumped into Yesenin and his
soft words, mingled with the throng that formed
around Pushkin or waited patiently at the Senate
Square while you threw pieces of Blok, Akhmatova
and poor old Mayakovsky to eager readers who
pecked at your references, I would come to
understand all that you represent.

But it was in St. Petersburg by the Kryucov where
the water flows down to the Neptune Arches that all
of European literature streams by, joins in your
verse, becomes a chorus for your song that is
steeped in old melodies, slow rhythms of centuries
gone by, the forgotten music of Ovid and Sappho
fills the air and the light grows stronger, the chorus
becomes an echo that carries the voices of Virgil
and Villon over the void pushing us forward and at
the same time calling us back to the magnificent
structures, the perfect poems that pass before us.

There was always the trap door, the false floor, and
falling through the mountain, the mist and the
morning after, and here on the open road a thimble
of Ariosto slipped into the cocktail so the readers
staggered past the sleeping guard as the camp fires
blossomed into fragrant flames and words that once
danced rose into the air tapping lightly on the ear so
that when he spoke of Homer his lines were salt sea
shells and foam and he never once had to say, "In
my youth I travelled with him."

At any moment he could hurl the ancient sand from another time, *The Divine Comedy* and Dante sting your eyes, you stumble onto the marketplace where poets hang their verses in brightly marked stalls and speak their poems in the language of the bluebird and the robin. There are a hundred voices calling out "I am the tour guide follow me" and this tug on your sleeve leads you down another street and further away from the end of Mandelstam's poem and deeper into the lush lands, the forgotten foothills of poetry and prose where the door to a locked century remains open.

Breathless I tried to keep up with him. I could hear the hoofs on the cobblestone and feel the sharpest points of literature piercing me and I loved that feeling and later I would pass my fingers over the page the way someone would run a hand over an old scar so that I could relive the moment when I was jarred out of my sleeping day and into the force of life.

The Last Poem
(Researcher's Notes #12)

When I came to his last poem I cried thinking this was the end. Days and nights, nights and days shuffled on. I too could have been someone or something but I stopped by this well to drink the last word, to watch the seasons change, and to unmask the fruit behind the thorns.

Here I lived, ate and slept waiting for the bluebirds to summon me each morning. I tallied up my emotions (with a small piece of chalk), felt the spears of sunlight through the clouds and anointed the words that had blessed me. And those ideas that returned home from their maiden voyage were restless and paced all night in the attic. Life was filled with the sounds of weightless feet in worn slippers and the threading thumbs and thimbles of spiders who laboured to reinforce the weakened dam of days that was flooding into years.

Sometimes in my sleep the poems tap me or flex their muscles as they push aside dreams. And then there is broken glass, ransacked images and streaks of lightning tethered to green strings, and finally a tune runs away with the words. Look! This was how I discovered the world was off course, by sinking with the ship, counting coral and holding on to his poems for dear life so that when I awoke in a country near the equator the words were stripped down to their meanings and oh how they carried themselves so erect so proud!

And now to say that the world went on, that laughter choked and almost died, that miracles were worked or postponed in a back room or a barn, that people swam in streams of blood, that my sister was called compassion and my brother was called something else is not important.

I am here on the other side of the century. Stalin is gone. Mandelstam's poems wave from mast heads and flag poles, leave fingerprints for visiting cards. They stretch out in open fields or sit in cafés where they trick tongues into leaping over borders, years and unmarked graves. To stop now is impossible, winter is coming, I wrap myself in a verse and head for the mountain pass where I can watch the poems as they migrate to the grazing lands.

NOTES

11   The translation of "Verses on the Unknown Soldier" is from *Osip Mandelstam: 50 Poems* (Persea Books, 1977), translator, Bernard Meares, introduction by Joseph Brodsky.

12   All quotations appearing in italics prior to a poem, as the title of a poem, or in the poem itself are fictitious.

17   Kibbutz Shamir is situated on the western slopes of the northern Golan Heights.

21   Primo Levi, *Moments of Reprieve* (Penguin Books, 1986), translator, Ruth Feldman.

28   3-5 Furmanov Street is the address in Moscow where the Mandelstams lived at the time of the poet's arrest.

30   The Lubyanka is the infamous political prison in Moscow where thousands were tortured and shot. It was also the headquarters for the secret police.

34   Nikolai Bukharin was a member of the Politburo from 1919 to 1929. He made two intercessions on Mandelstam's behalf to extricate the poet from dangerous situations. The later one, coming after Mandelstam's arrest, was a direct appeal to Stalin that most likely resulted in Mandelstam's life being spared and the poet being sent into exile. Bukharin was arrested in 1937, and shot on March 15, 1938.

37   Octavio Paz, *A Draft of Shadows* (New Directions Books, 1979), edited and translated by Eliot Weinberger.

44   Anna Akhmatova, one of the leading Russian poets of this period and a close friend of Mandelstam. She too was persecuted because of her poetry. Her poems were banned from publication, she was forced into poverty and her son was arrested twice and spent a total of fourteen years in prisons or camps. She visited the Mandelstams in Voronezh in February of 1936.

45   From Cynthia Ozic's introduction to *The Collected Stories of Isaac Babel* (Norton, 2002); editor, Nathalie Babel; translator, Peter Constantine.

53   *Hope Abandoned* (Atheneum, New York, and Collins and Harvill, London, 1973), translator, Max Hayward, is the second memoir written by Nadezhda Yakovlevna Mandelstam. The first, *Hope Against Hope* (Atheneum, New York, and Collins and Harvill,

London, 1970), translator, Max Hayward, provided me with a wealth of historical information and insights into the Mandelstams' lives for this book.

This translation of "Requiem" is from *The Complete Poems of Anna Akhmatova* (Zephyr Press, 2000), translator, Judith Hemschemeyer, edited and introduced by Roberta Reeder.

65   For the translation of Poem 227, see *Osip Mandelstam Selected Poems* (Penguin Books, 1991), translator, James Greene.

71   See above note for information on the translation of Poem 341.

The translation of Akhmatova's "The Wind of War" is the same as that for "Requiem," which is listed in the second note for p. 53.

74   The opening quote is a reference to Sophia Bogatyreva. She was only a schoolgirl when her father, Ignatij (Sania) Bershtein (pen name Aleksandr Ivich), and her mother, Nuria, took the great risk of housing the Mandelstam poems in their flat. A timely letter from her prior to my journey to Russia became an important touchstone with history for me while working on this book.

76   Natasha Shtempel befriended the Mandelstams during their exile in Voronezh. The Mandelstams entrusted her with copies of Osip's poems.

78   The name of this poem is a variation on the title of Mandelstam's prose piece "The Noise of Time."

The Cheka was the original name for the secret police.

79   The names mentioned in the first paragraph are the following famous Russian poets: Sergey Yesenin (1895–1925), Aleksandr Pushkin (1799–1837), Aleksandr Blok (1880–1921), Anna Akhmatova (1889–1966, see note for p. 40), and Vladimir Mayakovsky (1893–1930).

ACKNOWLEDGEMENTS

First to Maureen Whyte, the publisher of Seraphim Editions, for showing such enthusiasm for *Surviving the Censor*, and for allowing me to be involved in all the decisions pertaining to its publication.

To Allan Briesmaster, my editor, for displaying a remarkable understanding for what I was trying to achieve with this book and even greater patience with me as I wrote new poems and reworked old ones.

Jeff Bien's contribution to this book is immeasurable. He read and reread every poem, offering feedback, encouragement and honesty. He gave freely of his time over the course of a long illness and always at the expense of his own creative endeavours.

A.F. Moritz read *Surviving the Censor* in various forms on more than a few occasions and provided valuable suggestions.

Don Domanski worked on an earlier draft of this book with me during The Banff Centre for the Arts-Wired Writing Program.

The following people ensured that my literary pilgrimage to Russia was a success: Lena Astafieva, the Cultural Attaché at the Canadian Consulate, invited me to St. Petersburg to deliver the Alexander Mackenzie Memorial Lecture and organized my itinerary; Michael Wachtel, Professor of Slavic Languages and Literature at Princeton University, put me in contact with the Mandelstam Society and recommended Mandelstam specialists I should meet with, as did Sophia Bogatyreva (see the Notes for page 74); Dr. Alexsandre Mets and Sergei Vasilenko, two fine Mandelstam scholars, filled in all the gaps in my research; Leonid Vidgoff spent one magical day with me making Mandelstam's Moscow come alive and clarified points of Russian history and life after my trip was over.

To Michelle, Eli, Natacha, and my family, for their love, encouragement and understanding.